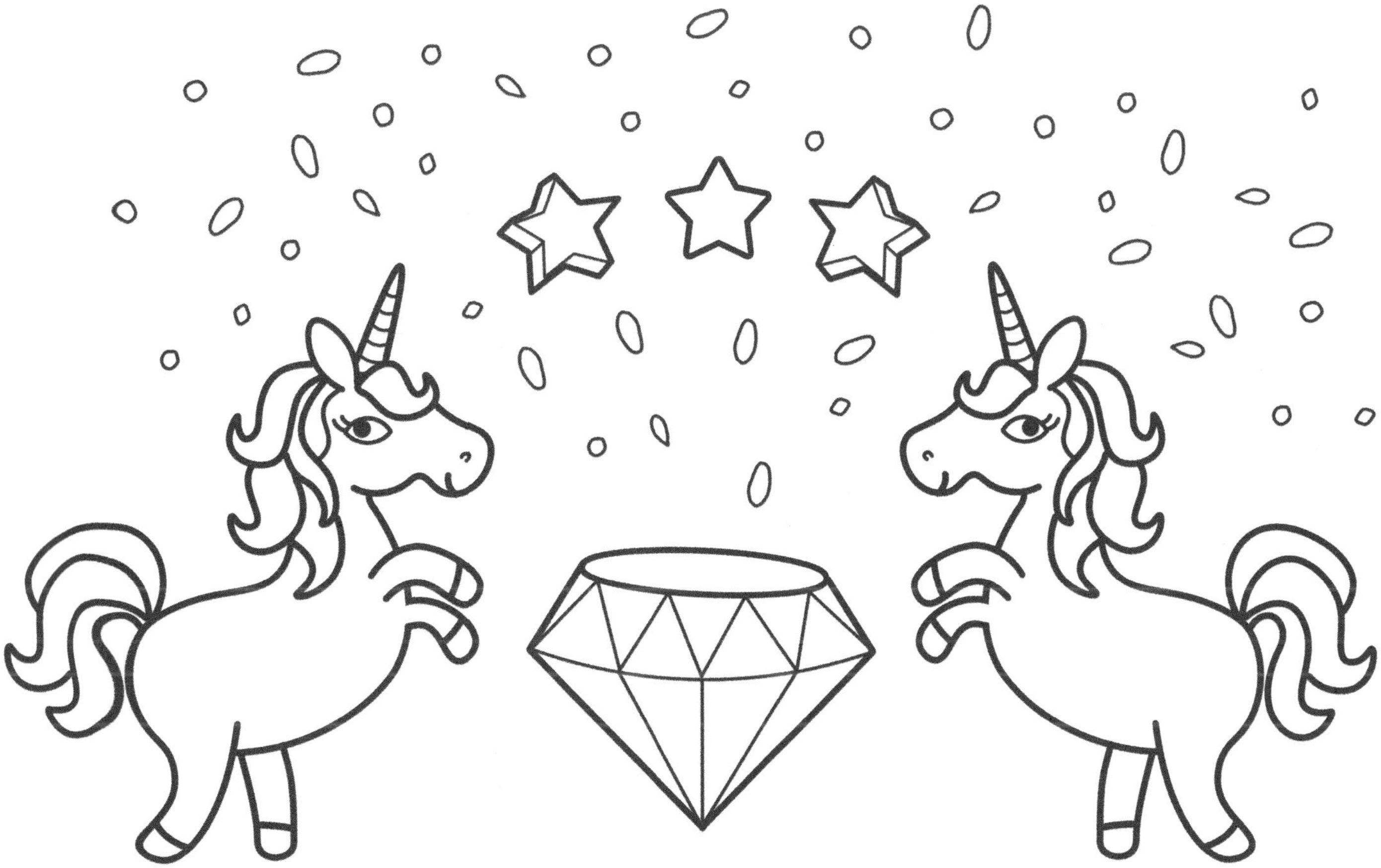

THIS BOOK BELONGS TO:

____

____

ISBN: 9781671977242

For more information and to stay updated on new coloring books visit our web site at
www.coloringbookkim.com

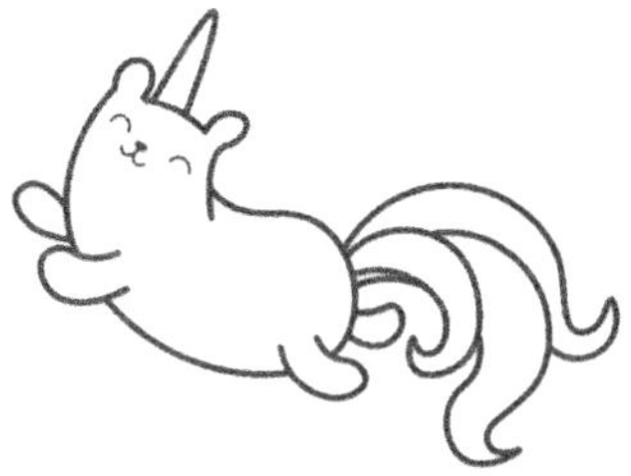

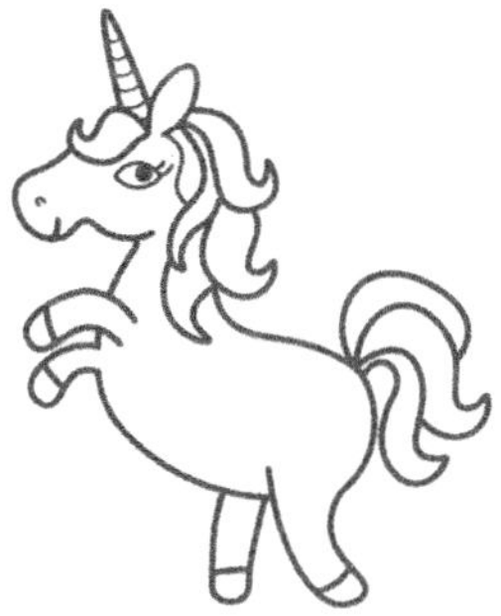

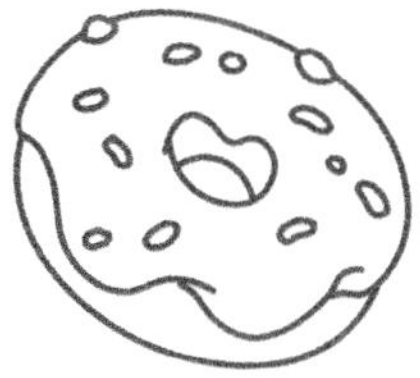

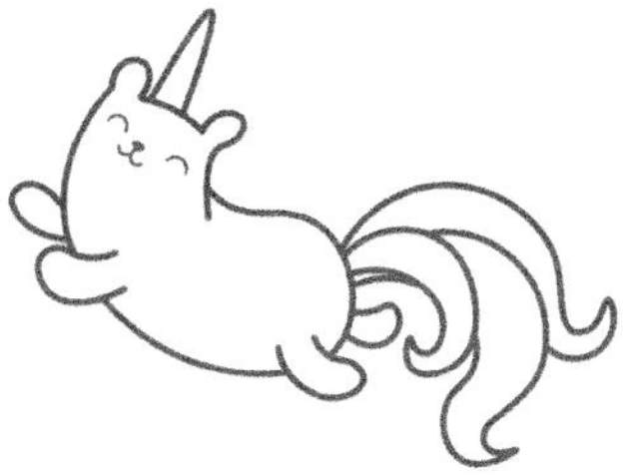

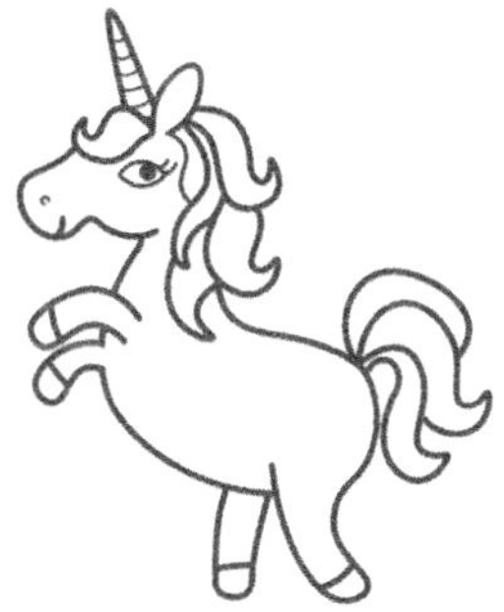

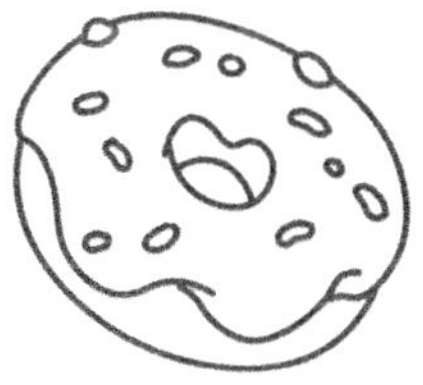

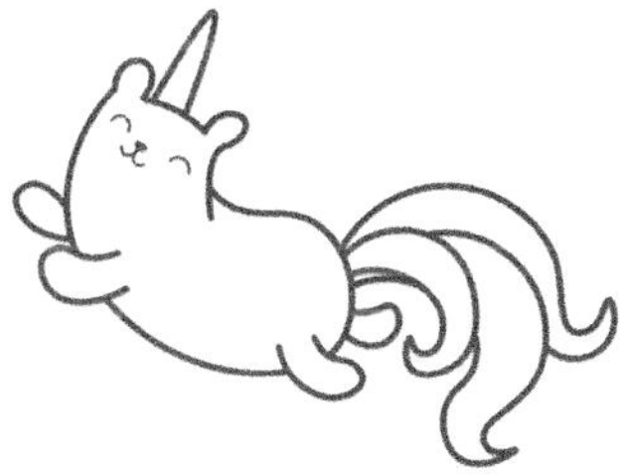

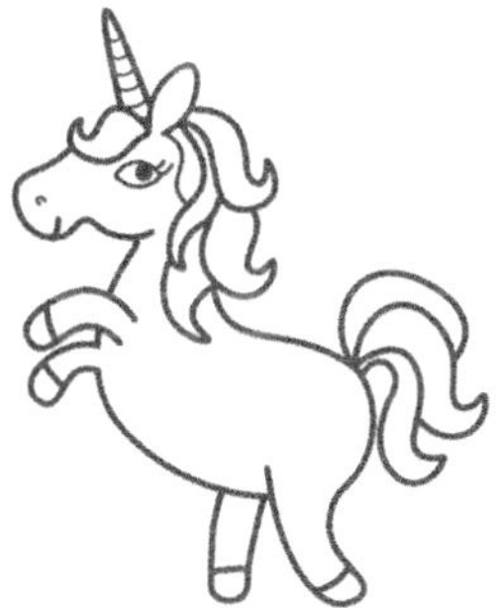

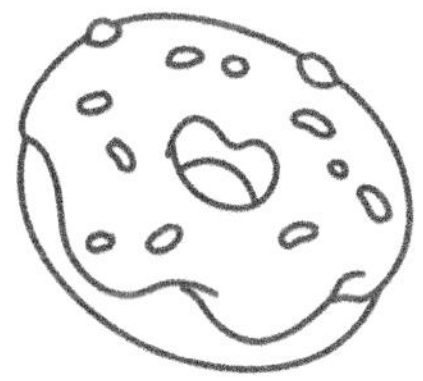

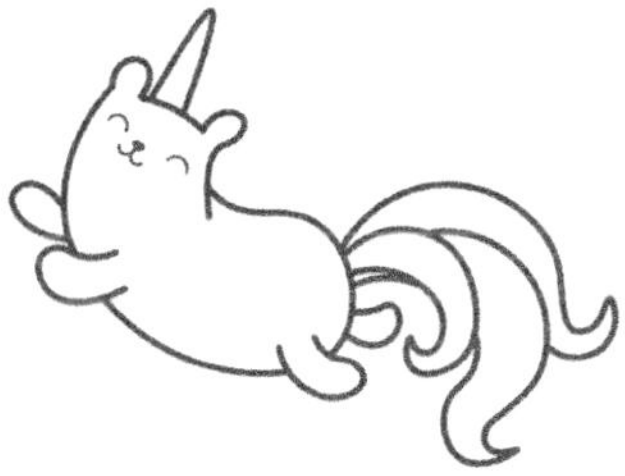

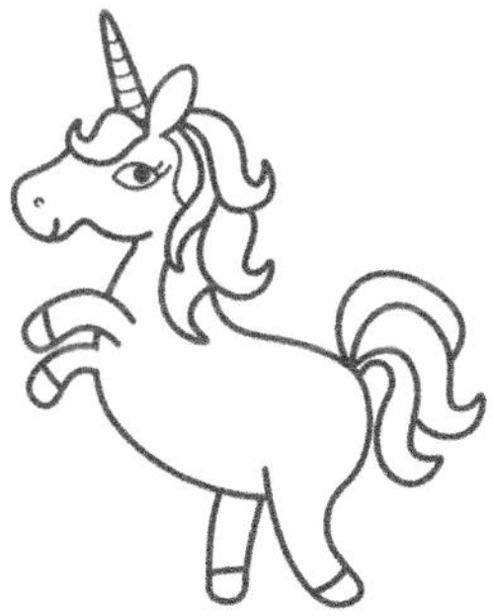

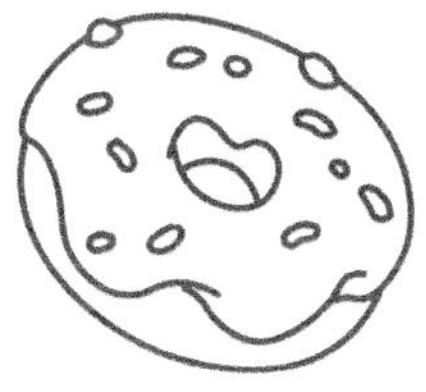

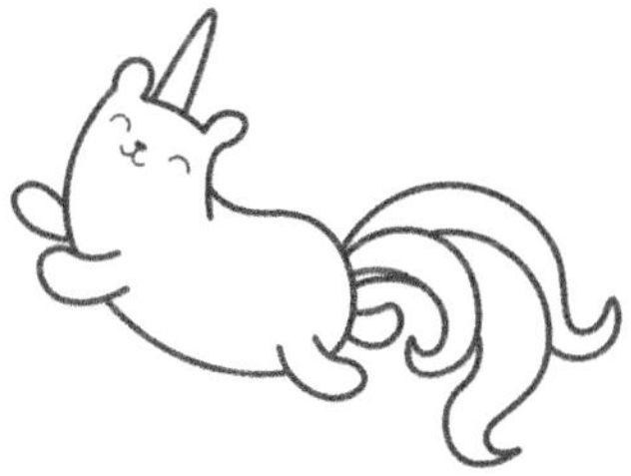

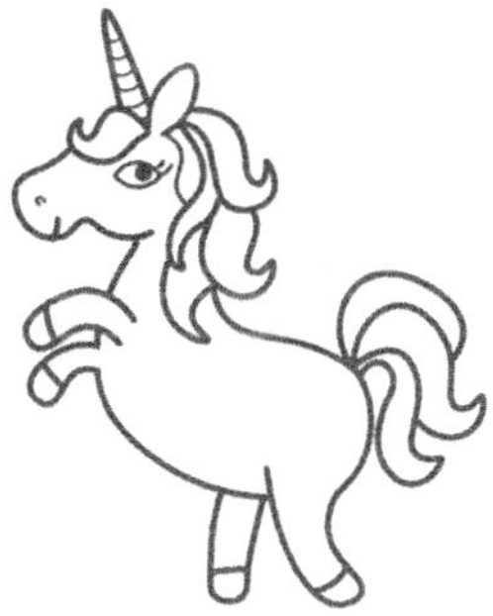

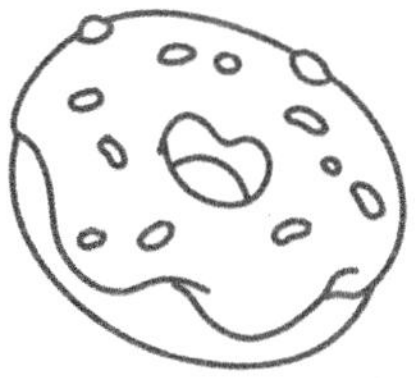

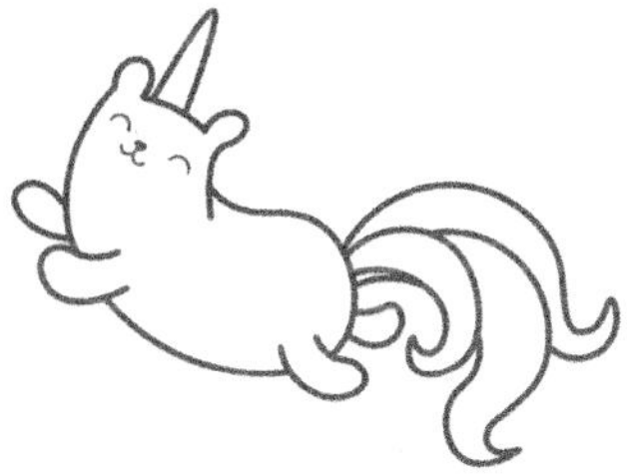

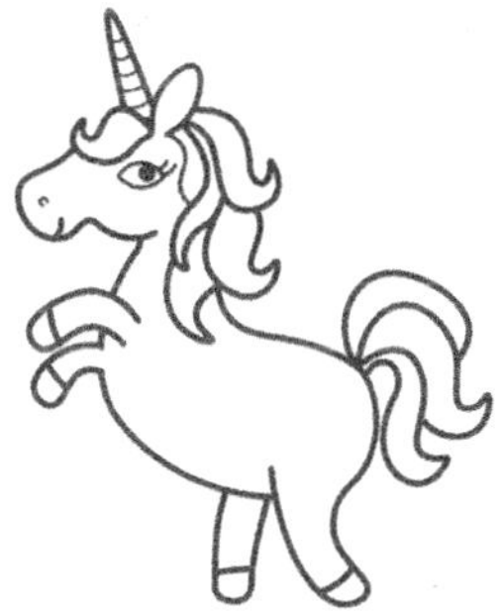

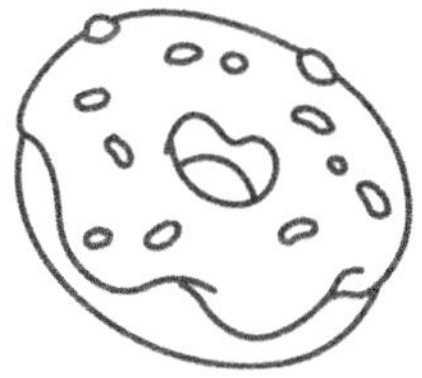

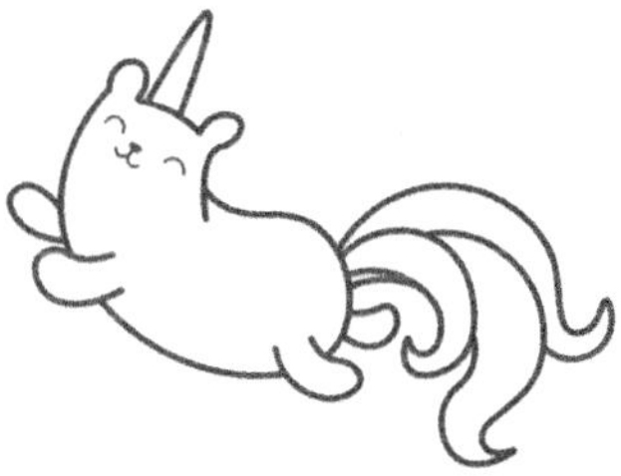

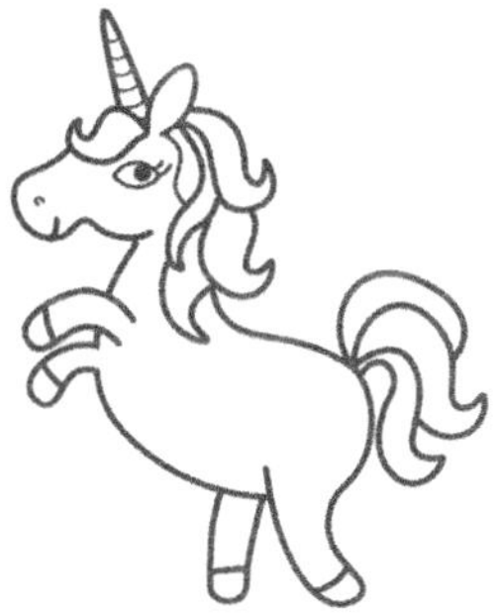

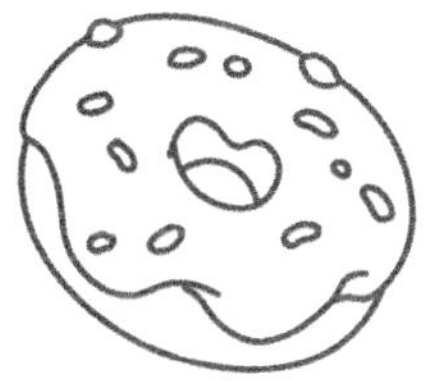

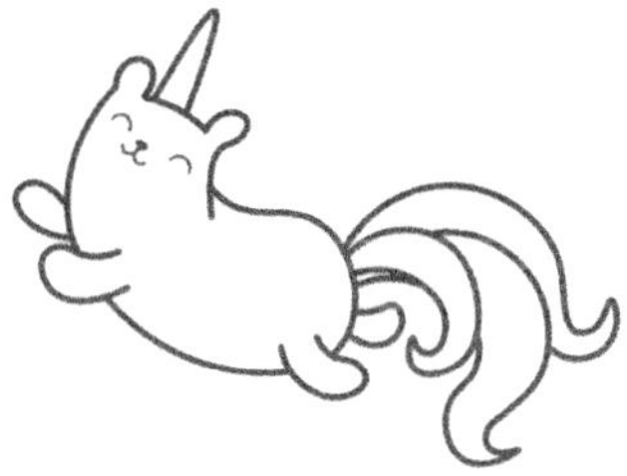

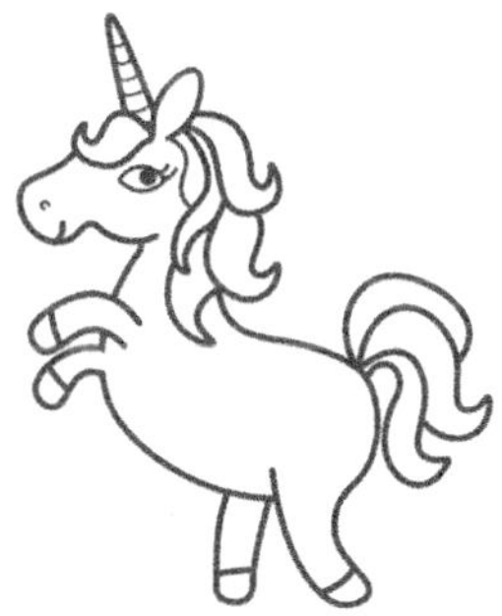

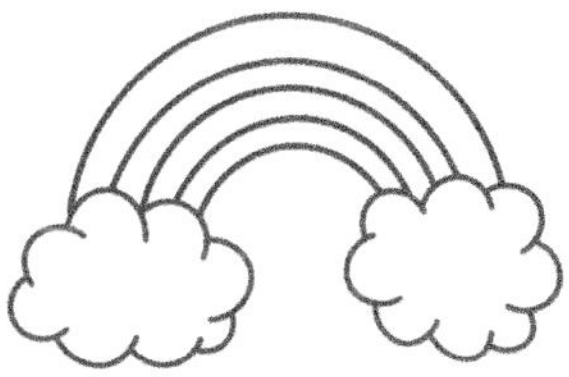

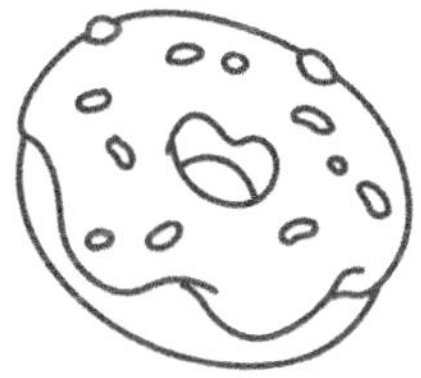

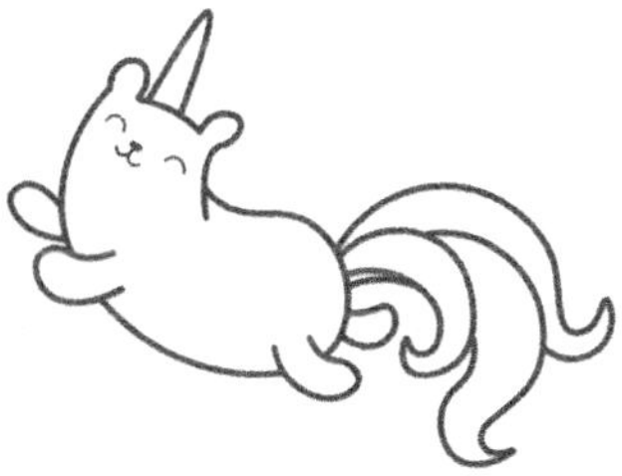

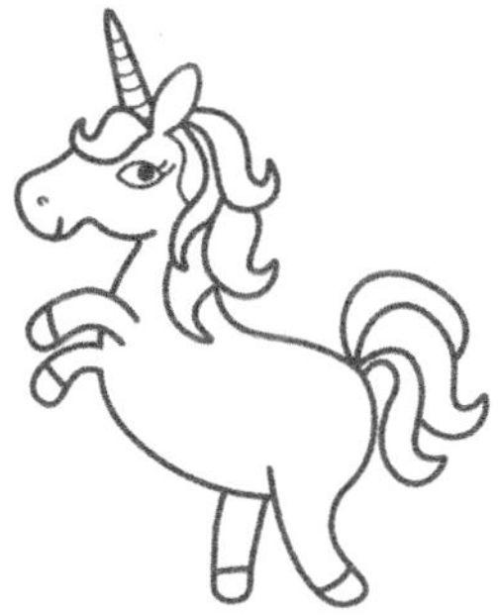

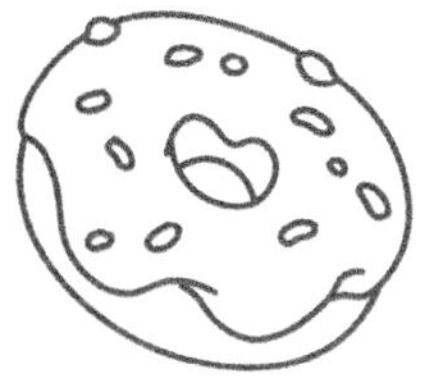

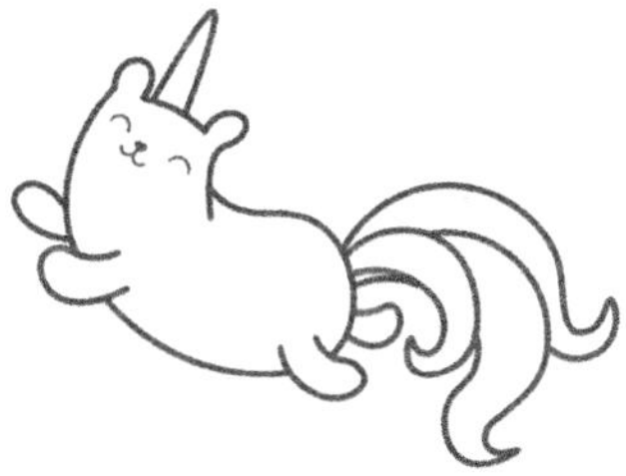

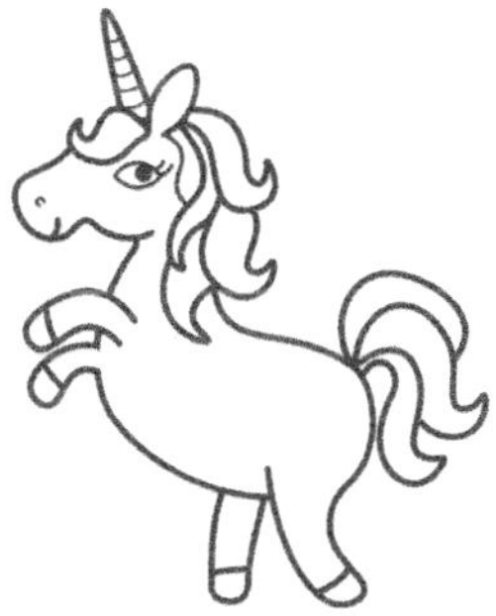

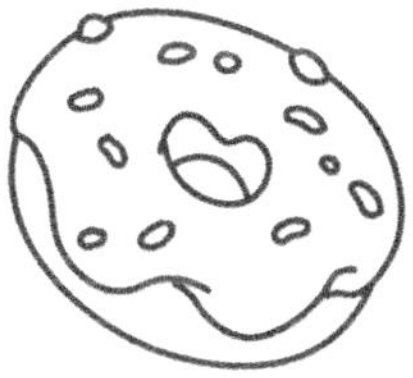

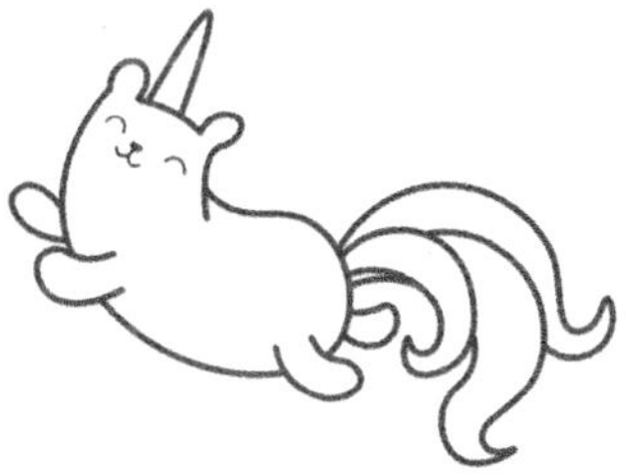

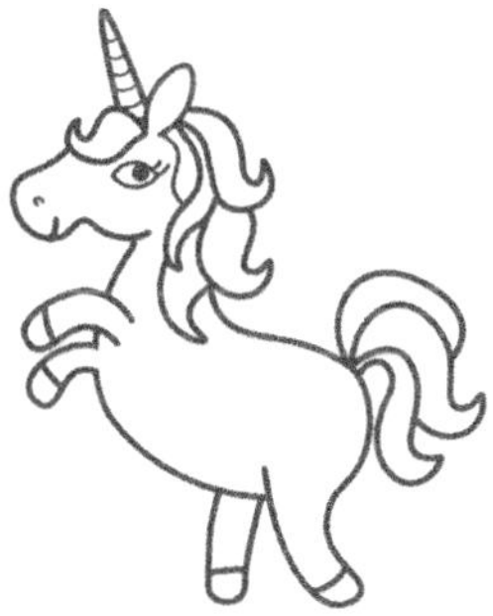

Made in the USA
Las Vegas, NV
15 December 2024

14288644R00063